Joint Implementation Plan

301-326 of the Dodd-Frank Wall Street Reform and Consumer Protection Act

January 2011
(Revised April 2011)

Board of Governors of the Federal Reserve System
Federal Deposit Insurance Corporation
Office of the Comptroller of the Currency
Office of Thrift Supervision

Washington, D.C.

Addendum
to
the Joint Implementation Plan, 301-326 of the Dodd-Frank Wall Street Reform and Consumer Protection Act, January 2011

This addendum amends the following paragraph from page 5 of the plan:

> *Upholding the protections afforded by the legislation.* The legislation provides a number of protections for transferred OTS employees. The agencies will ensure that employees are afforded the protections to which they are entitled.

to

> *Upholding the protections afforded by the legislation.* The legislation provides a number of protections for transferred OTS employees. The agencies will ensure that employees are afforded the protections to which they are entitled, including those required by section 322(g) of Dodd-Frank that prohibit involuntarily terminating a transferred individual's employment with the agency except for cause and involuntarily relocating employees except when that relocation is necessary for the efficient operation of the agency.

Table of Contents

1. *Overview*

This joint implementation plan has been prepared pursuant to section 327(a) of the Dodd-Frank Wall Street Reform and Consumer Protection Act, Public Law 111-203 (Dodd-Frank), and is submitted to the Committee on Banking, Housing, and Urban Affairs of the Senate, the Committee on Financial Services of the House of Representatives, and the Inspectors General of the Department of the Treasury, the Federal Deposit Insurance Corporation (FDIC), and the Board of Governors of the Federal Reserve Board (FRB). The FDIC, the FRB, the Office of the Comptroller of the Currency (OCC), and the Office of Thrift Supervision (OTS) jointly prepared this plan. It provides an overview of actions taken to date by the agencies to efficiently and effectively implement sections 301 through 326 of Dodd-Frank.

2. Transfer of Personnel

Section 2 describes the orderly transfer of personnel from the OTS to the OCC and the FDIC.

Pursuant to section 322(a) of Dodd-Frank, the Director of the OTS, the Comptroller of the Currency, and the FDIC Chairman will jointly determine the number of OTS employees necessary to perform and support the functions transferred to each agency. Pursuant to section 312(b)(2)(B) all of the OTS's functions relating to federal savings associations and all of the OTS's rulemaking authority for federal and state savings associations will be transferred to the OCC on the transfer date. Because these functions make up the bulk of the OTS's operations, most of the OTS's approximately 1,000 employees will transfer to the OCC. Senior managers from the OCC, the OTS, and the FDIC are meeting regularly to discuss the process and to identify the functions to transfer to each agency and the numbers of employees needed to perform and support those functions.

The OCC and the OTS have established transition teams to coordinate these efforts, and these teams are working together to identify and address mutual concerns and issues for resolution. The FDIC and the OTS are following a similar process. The OTS has shared information related to employee data, work locations, salary and classification structures, benefits, and human resources policies and practices with both the OCC and the FDIC. The human resources staffs of the three agencies have worked together to analyze this information, identify differences in policies and practices, assess implementation impacts, and formulate recommendations for the efficient and effective integration of their workforces.

Principles governing the transfer of personnel include:

- *Upholding the protections afforded by the legislation.* The legislation provides a number of protections for transferred OTS employees. The agencies will ensure that employees are afforded the protections to which they are entitled.

- *Building a sustainable organizational structure.* The OCC and the FDIC believe that integrating OTS staff and functions into the current organizational structures of the two agencies is the optimal solution to ensure that no gaps in supervision occur. The transferred OTS functions and staff will not constitute separate reporting lines of business in the OCC or the FDIC; rather, the agencies will integrate those individuals into their existing teams.

- *Fostering an environment that will maximize opportunities for staff.* The identification of the OTS staff who will transfer into the OCC and the FDIC will allow agency leadership to take advantage of the collective knowledge of combined staffs. Integrating staffs from the outset and equipping examiners with the training and skills necessary to examine both thrifts and banks will maximize opportunities for staff and will leverage the experience of both bank and thrift supervision regulators to support their missions.

- *Promoting communication to all employees throughout the transition.* A regular flow of information to OTS, FDIC, and OCC employees about the transition process is important to success. These agencies are providing ongoing communication to their employees to inform them of key implementation items and timelines, promote mission focus, and support a smooth transition.

2.1. Transferring Personnel

The first task for the agencies is to identify the primary OTS functions that will transfer to the OCC, the FDIC, and the FRB. Representatives from each agency are carefully reviewing the Dodd-Frank language to define the functions identified for transfer to the OCC, the FDIC, and the FRB. This information will help to determine the transfer of OTS staff to the OCC and the FDIC.

Pursuant to the legislation, the transfer of OTS employees must occur no later than 90 days after July 21, 2011.

As discussed below, OTS personnel transferring to the OCC and the FDIC will be placed into the OCC's and the FDIC's established pay systems and structures as soon as feasible following the date of transfer, but not later than 30 months after the transfer date as required by Dodd-Frank (section 322(j)). Other organizations that underwent similar transfers of personnel experienced significant delays and administrative burdens when maintaining two separate pay systems and structures, even if only for short periods following the transfer of functions and personnel. Both agencies have further determined that their current pay systems, with some possible modifications, can accommodate OTS's salary structure. However, the 30-month protection of pay may necessitate the retention of separate systems and structures for a period of time.

Personnel Transfers to the OCC. The OCC will assign OTS employees, to the extent practicable, to OCC positions performing the same functions and duties that the OTS employees performed prior to the transfer. The pay bands of these new positions will be based on established OCC standards for the classification of positions. While considerable differences exist, the agencies are working together to reach a consensus on how to integrate all OTS grades into the OCC pay bands.

Personnel Transfers to the FDIC. The FDIC plans a similar approach in integrating transferred staff into the existing FDIC organizational structure. The FDIC and the OTS have worked together to map their respective classification systems. The FDIC will ultimately use this tool to place OTS employees in comparable positions within the FDIC. In addition to establishing new positions for the transferring work, the FDIC is identifying existing vacancies that it might also use to place OTS employees. Available positions are being identified by location and grade, and the FDIC plans in early 2011 to solicit the interest of OTS employees in these vacancies. Final decisions on the transfer and placement of individual OTS employees will be made jointly by the FDIC and OTS.

Notice Commitments. The OCC and the FDIC intend to provide initial notification letters to transferring employees and meet with them as soon as possible, but not later than 60 days before the transfer date. Initial notices will describe: (a) how the transfer will occur, (b) the actual date of the transfer, (c) information on affecting the transfer through a personnel action, (d) the corresponding "grade" level, (e) duty location, (f) tentative organizational assignment, and (g)available information on the position assignment. In addition to the written notification, the agencies will use a variety of communication channels to ensure that employees are aware of the decisions and opportunities that affect them. Consistent with the legislation, final notification of position assignments with full details will follow no later than 120 days after the effective date of each employee's transfer. The OCC intends to effect these changes by the transfer date.

The OTS will provide regular updates to the OCC and the FDIC regarding current personnel to ensure that both agencies are aware of changes due to retirements, transfers, resignations, or other actions. This information will ensure that each agency maintains accurate rosters through the transfer date.

The OCC and the FDIC are also monitoring other aspects related to the transfer of OTS personnel. For example, the OCC will provide a roster of transferred employees to the OCC's manager of payroll systems and to the OCC's manager of other financial systems (such as travel, time/attendance, and work reports). These managers are working with their OTS counterparts and with the payroll service provider, the National Finance Center (NFC), to manage the transfer within appropriate systems. The OCC and the OTS also are meeting weekly with the NFC and the Department of the Treasury's HRConnect Program Office (administrator of OCC's and OTS's human resources systems) to ensure a smooth transition from OTS's payroll and personnel systems. NFC is also the FDIC's payroll provider, but the FDIC has a separate human resources system (Corporate Human Resources Information System or CHRIS).

The OCC and FDIC business units also are coordinating with their OTS counterparts to review positions, responsibilities, and business processes to determine the best means of integrating staff and their functions into the OCC and the FDIC. A thorough review of OTS position descriptions is necessary for this exercise.

2.2. Safeguards To Ensure OTS Employees Are Not Unfairly Disadvantaged

The OCC and the FDIC are committed to ensuring that transferred OTS employees receive equitable treatment with respect to their status, tenure, pay, benefits and accrued leave or vacation time for prior periods of service with a federal agency, as required in section 322(e) and section 322(k)(2) of Dodd-Frank. The OCC and the FDIC also intend to properly document all decisions regarding position and organizational assignments of transferred employees to ensure that every transferred employee is accounted for, aligned properly into the OCC or the FDIC, and retains the same pay, status, and tenure, and to the extent practicable, functions and duties, in effect immediately preceding the effective date of the transfer.

Both OCC and FDIC leadership and human resources personnel have worked with their OTS counterparts to review human resources policies, identify gaps and differences in those policies, and assess impacts of those differences. Based on this analysis, the OCC and the FDIC plan to continue existing human resources policies. The two agencies will consider future changes to policies where they benefit the combined organizations and their employees. No changes will be adopted that in any way result in an unfair disadvantage to transferred employees. The agencies recognize the importance of providing employees the protections afforded to them by Dodd-Frank and continue to work on details regarding safeguarding pay, tenure, and status as well as continuing to discuss details regarding position assignments of managers who transfer from the OTS to OCC and issues regarding examiner accreditation and training requirements.

As required by section 322(k)(4) of Dodd-Frank, the OCC and the FDIC will submit a study to Congress within 365 days after the transfer date describing and demonstrating the procedures and safeguards adopted by the agencies to ensure that they meet the requirements of section 322(k).

2.3. Protection of Pay, Status, Tenure, Functions, and Duties

Section 322(e) of Dodd-Frank requires that the OCC and the FDIC place each transferred employee in a position with the same status, tenure, and to the extent practicable, functions and duties as the transferred employee held on the day before the date on which the employee was transferred. In addition, for 30 months beginning on the date the employee is transferred, the employee shall be paid at a rate not less than the basic rate of pay (including geographic differential) that the employee received during the pay period immediately preceding the date on which the employee was transferred.

If the salary of the transferred employee exceeds the pay range of the position in which placed, the OCC and the FDIC will provide saved pay to ensure the employees' pay is not adversely affected. In accordance with Dodd-Frank, neither the OCC nor the FDIC will reduce a transferred employee's pay during the 30-month period except in the limited circumstances specifically permitted by Dodd-Frank.

2.4. Protection and Continuation of Retirement Benefits

The majority of OCC, FDIC, and OTS employees participate in one of two retirement systems administered by the Office of Personnel Management (OPM)—the Civil Service Retirement System (CSRS) and the Federal Employees Retirement System (FERS). A portion of OTS's current employees participate in a third retirement system, the Financial Institutions Retirement Fund (FIRF). FIRF is a defined benefit plan administered by Pentegra Retirement Services (Pentegra).

A defined benefit plan is a pension plan that provides a specific payment based on a formula that combines salary and years of service. Unlike CSRS and FERS, FIRF is a system where all costs are paid by the employer (in this case, OTS) into one general account. At retirement, employees may either receive a lump sum or opt for an annuity/lump sum split. The employee must elect to receive at least 25 percent of their distribution as an annuity in order to continue receiving an annuity benefit. Early and optional retirement ages under FIRF are different from those of CSRS and FERS. Approximately 375 current OTS employees participate in FIRF, and approximately 460 retirees receive a FIRF annuity.

Because the OTS serves as the benefit administrator for OTS retirees—much like the OPM serves as the CSRS and FERS benefit administrator for federal agencies—the OCC will assume that same benefit administrator role on the transfer date. The OCC has also agreed to provide retirement benefits administration for OTS/FIRF employees who transfer to the FDIC and the Bureau of Consumer Financial Protection. Agencies receiving transferred OTS employees will make payroll and financial systems adjustments similar to those of the OCC to accommodate FIRF entitlements of these transferred OTS employees and will coordinate with the OCC to ensure integrated benefits delivery to these employees. The OCC will maintain continuity by using transferred OTS staff members with the expertise to oversee FIRF and its contract with Pentegra to the greatest extent possible. The OCC will modify its financial systems to accommodate any additional transactions required to support FIRF entitlements. The OCC also will modify payroll systems to include an OTS/FIRF identifier to ensure that the OCC makes accurate contributions to the FIRF account. NFC is the current payroll provider for the OTS and is already familiar with the FIRF deduction process. Regular audits will ensure that transferred employees maintain their coverage in FIRF.

The OCC is committed to adhering to sound financial policies and management oversight of FIRF to ensure FIRF's sustainability for current and future retirees.

Transferred OTS employees covered by CSRS or FERS will remain in those retirement systems.

2.5. Supplemental Retirement Benefits

Both the OCC and the FDIC have additional retirement savings programs for their employees that will be available to transferred OTS employees. The following is a description of those programs and how transferred employees may participate and roll over OTS-unique retirement savings programs into these programs.

Both the OCC and the FDIC provide qualified retirement savings plans in the form of a 401(k) program to their employees. The plans offer an additional opportunity to save and invest for the future. Although employee contribution options are similar, employer matching and vesting policies differ. Both agencies contract out to separate private vendors to administer the program, with oversight provided by the agencies and an internal committee of employees and managers. Both have similar accounts for employees (e.g., regular 401(k), Roth, etc.). In accordance with section 322(i) of Dodd-Frank, the supplemental retirement benefits of OTS employees will continue as provided for by law.

2.6. Protection and Continuation of Benefits Other than Retirement

The OCC and the FDIC offer benefits programs similar to those of the OTS, but with some notable differences. Human resource specialists from the OCC, the FDIC, and the OTS have completed a side-by-side analysis comparing the benefits programs of the three agencies. The highlights follow:

- The OCC offers the following agency-paid programs not offered by the OTS: Dental Insurance, Vision Insurance, Tamiflu Protection, Physical Exam Program, and a health unit at Headquarters. The FDIC provides Dental and Vision Insurance at minimal cost to employees in addition to providing Tamiflu Protection and a health unit at Headquarters, like the OCC.
- The OCC offers the following employee-paid programs not offered by the OTS or the FDIC: 24-Hour Personal Accident Insurance, and Short Term Disability Insurance.
- Both the OCC and the OTS offer a Lifecycle Account Program, which the FDIC does not offer. The OTS offers a Lifecycle Account Program with a greater benefit than the OCC.
- Both the OCC and the FDIC offer a Parking Flexible Spending Account not offered by the OTS.
- Both the OCC and the FDIC offer agency-paid Business Travel Accident Insurance with higher coverage levels than the OTS.
- Both the FDIC and the OTS offer agency-paid Group Life Insurance with higher coverage levels than the OCC, especially for executives. The OTS and the FDIC offer the following programs with benefits greater than the OCC: Long Term Disability Insurance, Military Reservist Protections, and Wellness Screenings.
- Both the OCC and the FDIC offer Domestic Partner Benefits at greater levels than the OTS. Both the FDIC and the OCC offer domestic partners (same and opposite sex) dental, vision and dependent life insurance coverage, a health insurance premium subsidy, business travel accident insurance, and relocation benefits.
- The following programs are comparable at the three agencies: Federal Employees Health Benefits (FEHB), Federal Employees Group Life Insurance, and employee-paid programs—Long Term Care insurance and the Federal Employees Dental and Vision Insurance Program (federal dental and vision insurance).
- All three agencies provide a comparable FEHB premium subsidy.
- The FDIC offers a Flexible Spending Account with no government contribution. The OTS provides a $1,000 contribution, which can be deposited in either a flexible spending

account (pre-tax) or the Lifecycle Account (post-tax). OCC employees may choose to deposit their $900 lifecycle benefit into their flexible spending account pre-tax.

- The OCC, the OTS, and the FDIC offer separate 401(k) plans. The FDIC plan has the highest agency contribution, allowing for a five percent employer match of contributions, whereas the OCC contributes three percent and the OTS four percent. In addition, under the FDIC and the OCC Savings Plans, contributions can be made pre-tax or after-tax (Roth).

Section 322(i) of Dodd-Frank provides that transferred OTS employees may retain their benefits for the one-year period following the transfer date. The OCC and the FDIC have carefully compared their respective benefits packages to those of the OTS and considered the possibility of offering OTS employees the choice of remaining in the OTS benefits program or moving into the benefits program of the agency to which they are transferred (the OCC or the FDIC). However, both agencies have decided to leave the transferred OTS employees in the OTS benefits programs as currently constituted for the first year after transfer. This decision not only complies with the requirements of the legislation but ensures that the agencies have sufficient time to work through related systems and contracting issues associated with integrating the two benefits programs.

2.6.1. Continuation of Health, Dental, Vision, Long-Term Care Insurance

Consistent with Dodd-Frank, transferred employees will remain in their federal programs and continue to receive the current OTS FEHB subsidy for the first year following the transfer. After one year, all employees will transition to OCC and FDIC benefit programs.

2.6.2. Continuation of Life Insurance Benefits

For employees transferring to the OCC and the FDIC, transferred employees will remain in the OTS benefits programs as currently constituted for the first year following the transfer. The FDIC and the OCC will jointly explore options for the most efficient administration of this separate OTS benefit program during this interim period. After such time, all employees will transition to OCC and FDIC benefit programs or other federal benefit programs offered to all federal employees.

2.7. Incorporation into Agency Pay Systems

Section 322(h) of Dodd-Frank provides OTS employees pay protection during the 30-month period after each employee is transferred to the OCC or the FDIC. Transferred employees will be paid at a rate that is not less than the basic rate of pay, including any geographic differential that the transferred employees received during the pay period immediately preceding the date the employee is transferred.

2.7.1. Incorporation into the OCC Pay System

The pay structures-of the OCC and the OTS differ significantly. The OCC has a nine-band pay system, with bands VIII and IX regarded as the executive level. Minimum and maximum salaries are set within each band, and salaries are adjusted based on merit. Band salaries are considered base pay. Annually, the OCC surveys the Financial Institutions Reform, Recovery and Enforcement Act (FIRREA) agencies to determine what adjustments it should make to ensure comparability with these agencies, as required by FIRREA. Additionally, the agency uses geographic pay differentials, considered separately from base pay, when the OCC finds significant differences in living and/or labor costs for various metropolitan areas. Nevertheless, benefit computations include base pay plus any geographic differential.

The OTS has a 30-grade pay system, with grades 25-30 regarded as the executive level. Salary ranges include a minimum, midpoint, and maximum. The OTS also annually reviews and compares salaries against other FIRREA agencies. The OTS collects cost-of-living data for the locations in which employees are assigned to determine geographic pay differentials. Unlike the OCC, the OTS does not separate base pay into salary and geographic adjustment. Because salary structures are adjusted to reflect geographic differences in the cost of living, the OTS considers the employee's full salary as base pay for all compensation computations. Both organizations use the higher number for benefits computations.

Even with these noted differences, the OCC salary structure can accommodate the transfer of all employees from the OTS salary structure. Moving to one agency pay system as soon as feasible after the transfer date will support early and successful integration. Section 322(j) of Dodd-Frank requires the agencies to complete this transition within 30 months of the transfer date. The OCC will assign OTS employees to OCC positions in accordance with section 322(e) of Dodd-Frank. When a transferred employee's salary fits within the assigned OCC pay band range for the assigned position, the OCC will set the salary within that OCC pay band and at the same level the transferred employee received during the pay period immediately prior to the effective date of the transfer. Where a transferred employee's salary exceeds the OCC pay band range for the position assignment, the OCC will assure that the pay protection required by Dodd-Frank is invoked and applied accordingly.

The OCC and the OTS compensation policies and mechanisms for permanent adjustments to base pay and other types of pay increases also differ. The OCC will maintain its human resources policies, including compensation, merit increases, and merit bonuses to recognize and incentivize performance. At the same time, the OCC continues to work closely with OTS human resources professionals to identify and resolve differences in these policies with an eye toward considering future changes that will benefit the combined organization and its employees.

2.7.2. Incorporation into the FDIC Pay System

The pay-for-performance systems of the FDIC and the OTS also differ significantly. The FDIC has a 15-grade Corporate Grade (CG) structure (similar to the General Schedule) for non-supervisory employees; two Corporate Manager (CM) pay bands for supervisory and managerial employees; a Corporate Expert (CX) pay band for senior, non-supervisory technical experts; and an Executive Management (EM) pay band for executive level employees. The EM and CX bands include positions equivalent to the SES. Minimum and maximum salaries are set for each grade/pay band. Like the OCC, FDIC salaries include two components, base salary and a locality pay adjustment. The latter is determined separately from base pay to compensate for significant differences in labor and/or living costs for various metropolitan areas. Benefits computations are based on base pay plus locality pay.

Like the OCC and the OTS, the FDIC participates annually in a joint survey of the FIRREA agencies to determine what adjustments it should make to ensure comparability with these agencies. However, the FDIC negotiates pay and benefits with its employee union, and pay and benefits for its bargaining unit employees are typically covered by multi-year negotiated compensation agreements.

Despite the differences between the FDIC and the OTS classification and pay systems, the FDIC is confident that its salary structures can, with limited adjustments, accommodate the OTS salary structures. As with the OCC, the FDIC plans to convert transferred OTS employees to its pay system as soon as feasible after the transfer date and well before the 30-month deadline established by Dodd-Frank. The FDIC will map existing OTS positions to the FDIC classification and pay system as quickly as possible. Where a transferred employee's salary fits within the assigned FDIC pay range, the FDIC will set the salary at the same level within that FDIC pay grade; where a transferred employee's salary exceeds the maximum salary for the assigned FDIC pay range, the FDIC will maintain the employee's higher salary in accordance with the requirements of Dodd-Frank.

Mechanisms for permanent adjustments to base pay and other types of pay increases at the FDIC and the OTS also differ. The FDIC will maintain its established policies regarding performance-based base pay increases and bonuses/lump sum payments to recognize and incentivize performance. At the same time, the FDIC will work with OTS human resources professionals as needed to identify and resolve differences in these policies with an eye toward considering future changes that will benefit the combined organization and its employees. Such changes may also require negotiations with the FDIC's employee union.

3. *Transfer of Authority and Responsibilities*

Section 3 of this plan describes the orderly transfer of authority and responsibilities to provide effective and efficient supervision of the thrift industry. It describes the steps the agencies are taking to transfer the responsibilities of supervising federal savings associations to the OCC, state savings associations to the FDIC, and savings and loan holding companies to the FRB. This section outlines steps taken to ensure personnel are adequately trained and equipped to perform these responsibilities.

3.1. *Transfer of Authority and Responsibilities Regarding Oversight of Federal Savings Associations*

Pursuant to section 312(b)(2)(B) all of the OTS's functions relating to federal savings associations, of which there will be approximately 670 on the transfer date, and all of the OTS's rulemaking authority for federal and state savings associations will be transferred to the OCC on the transfer date. Because these functions make up the bulk of the OTS's operations, most OTS personnel and assets will transfer to the OCC. Although the legislation preserves the federal thrift charter and the Home Owners' Loan Act (HOLA), it abolishes the OTS 90 days after the transfer date.

The OCC is working with the OTS to execute an orderly transfer of authority and responsibilities that will ensure the effective supervision of both national banks and federal savings associations. The OCC developed the following set of principles to guide the supervision integration strategy:

1. Build a sustainable staffing structure that provides flexibility through the transition.

2. Uphold the protections afforded by the legislation and maximize opportunities for staff.

3. Fully and quickly integrate thrifts and OTS staff into the OCC supervision model, including problem bank supervision.

4. Preserve the single Deputy Comptroller model in each OCC district and department to ensure clear leadership.

5. Preserve the benefits of a flat organizational structure, including bank supervision decision-making authority.

6. Ensure a reasonable span of control for managers with the additional thrift supervision workload.

7. Minimize disruption to staff, processes, and industry.

8. Minimize the number of new office locations.

9. Over time, have employees live where the work is located.

10. Over time, ensure each commissioned examiner has the skill set and credentials to supervise both thrifts and banks.

11. Deploy staff consistent with the OCC's integrated staffing strategy. The OCC will assign the majority of staff to the districts and the OCC's Community Bank Supervision program, but will deploy examiner resources across business lines to also fulfill priorities in the OCC's Midsize and Large Bank Supervision programs.

12. Assign larger federal saving associations to the OCC's Midsize and Large Bank Supervision portfolios based on business model and geographic footprint.

Using these principles, OCC management developed a range of options for restructuring and discussed these options with the National Treasury Employees Union (NTEU) representatives and OTS senior management. Feedback from the NTEU and the OTS helped shape the final recommendation approved by the OCC Executive Committee. The OCC believes that the following decisions are fully consistent with the 12 guiding principles above and will ensure high quality, effective supervision for national banks and federal savings associations. The details of these decisions were discussed with staff at the OTS and the OCC on December 7, 2010.

Throughout the transition, the agencies will take care to minimize disruption to the industry while implementing best practices in bank supervision. The more than 1,300 nationally chartered community banks that the OCC currently supervises use a variety of business models, including a significant number of institutions that look very similar to thrifts with a preponderance of long-term assets. The OCC also supervises other types of specialized institutions, including credit card banks and trust banks. Because of this diversity of experience, OCC examiners understand the importance of evaluating the condition and future prospects of each institution based on its unique characteristics and performance, as well as its local market conditions.

The OCC's objective is to complete an orderly transfer of OTS authority and responsibilities by fully and quickly integrating OTS staff and functions into the current OCC organizational structure and supervisory model. The functions relating to supervision of federal savings associations and the staff from the OTS who supervise these institutions will not constitute a separate reporting line of business in the organization.

The OCC and OTS staff currently participate in some of the other agency's supervisory reviews of problem banks. Starting in early 2011, the OCC and OTS will jointly develop fiscal year 2012 examination plans and supervisory strategies for federal savings associations and will conduct a small number of pilot examinations on a joint basis.

OCC's Community Bank Supervision will supervise the vast majority of federal savings associations. The Special Supervision portfolio will expand to include certain troubled federal savings associations. Midsize and Large Bank Supervision programs will supervise federal savings associations with profiles that align with those units.

The OCC's Community Bank Supervision function will continue with four districts and will be led by the existing Deputy Comptrollers. Each District Deputy Comptroller's span of control will increase by more than 50 percent on average with the addition of a significant number of federal savings associations and OTS examiners. To compensate for that realignment, the OCC is creating a new management position titled "Associate Deputy Comptroller" (AsDC). AsDCs will be located in each district office (two each in Northeast, Central, and Western; and three in the Southern District) and will report to the Deputy Comptroller for those districts. The AsDCs will supervise the Assistant Deputy Comptrollers (ADCs) and will be supported by analysts. This structure will allow the Deputy Comptrollers to focus on leadership, strategy, development of staff, and rapid integration of federal savings associations and OTS staff. The addition of the AsDCs will result in a more manageable portfolio distribution, enhance the management succession pool, and facilitate prompt consultation on supervision and personnel issues.

For Midsize Bank Supervision, the OCC will add two AsDC positions (one in Chicago and one in Washington, D.C.).

The OCC also will add a Senior Advisor for Thrift Supervision (Senior Thrift Advisor) in each district office reporting directly to the Deputy Comptroller. The Senior Thrift Advisor will be an expert resource on thrift supervision, serving as a key member of the District Deputy Comptroller's senior management team that provides advice, support, and leadership in all aspects of district operations. In addition, the OCC will establish a Senior Thrift Advisor position in Special Supervision reporting to the Deputy Comptroller. In addition to the duties described in section 3.1.1, the recently named Deputy Comptroller for Thrift Supervision will serve as an advisor for the Midsize and Large Bank Supervision portfolios.

Under the new structure, ADCs will maintain their existing authorities and responsibilities. To address the increase in institutions and staff, the OCC will add ADC and Team Leader positions, as needed. In some locations, the OCC will have substantial increases in staff but not institutions. In those cases, the agency plans to use an ADC for Resource Management. The ADC for Resource Management may have some bank portfolio responsibilities but will focus primarily on the effective deployment of examiners to facilitate implementation of the district business plans, including support of Midsize and Large Bank Supervision resource needs. The tentative list of new ADC positions includes:

- Northeast: Boston, Charlotte, New York Metro (2), Philadelphia, Pittsburgh, and Wilkes Barre/Washington, D.C.

- Southern: Atlanta (Resource), Dallas (Resource), Jacksonville, and New Orleans

- Central: Chicago North, Cincinnati, Cleveland, Indianapolis, Minneapolis, and St Louis

- Western: California (Resource), Des Moines, Kansas City, and Seattle

- Midsize: Chicago and Washington, D.C.

Des Moines and Seattle represent new field office locations for the OCC. To accommodate the increase in staff and the new ADC positions, the OCC is working to determine space requirements. The OCC plans to minimize disruption to employees and the work they perform, and optimize existing OCC and OTS office space as available. Consequently, the OCC will carefully manage the staffing of various offices, taking into consideration the necessary work, expiration of office leases, the capacity of existing offices to absorb additional staff, the impact of office locations and assignments on travel requirements and work-life balance for employees, and other relevant factors.

The remaining positions created by the OCC's structural changes will be posted for internal competition and qualified OTS and OCC staff will be encouraged to apply. The OCC will post the new management positions in sequence (AsDC and Senior Thrift Advisor first, followed by the ADC and Team Leader positions) beginning in the first quarter of calendar year 2011. The related analyst positions will be posted following the management selections.

Similar to the supervision functions, other OCC organizations are working to integrate transferring OTS employees into those functional organizations.

3.1.1. Designation of a Deputy Comptroller for Thrift Supervision (OCC)

Pursuant to section 314(b) of Dodd-Frank, on November 3, 2010, the OCC designated a Deputy Comptroller for Thrift Supervision. He will lead the planning process for integration of the OTS's examination and supervision functions and staff, serve as a key senior management group member, coordinate the nationwide network of Senior Thrift Advisors, function as the key advisor to other Deputy Comptrollers on large and problem thrifts, and will report to the Senior Deputy Comptroller for Midsize/Community Bank Supervision.

3.1.2. Training and Certification of Employees (OCC)

Training will be critical to the combined success of the OCC and the OTS. The agencies are reviewing each of their training and certification programs to ensure that existing and transferred employees have the training and skills necessary to supervise both national banks and federal savings associations. This review will identify where OCC and OTS training programs overlap and where gaps need to be addressed. While the legislation does not require additional certification for transferred OTS employees to continue supervising the types of institutions that they supervised prior to the transfer, additional training may be required before transferred employees may supervise other types of institutions. The expectation is that on and after the transition date, all examiners who serve as Examiner in Charge (EIC) of thrifts or banks will continue to perform these functions.

Following the transfer date, the OCC will ensure that bank and thrift examiners conducting bank and thrift supervision have the necessary expertise to meet the challenge of supervising new types of institutions. The OCC has engaged a consultant to identify any differences between the OTS examiner accreditation process and the OCC's Uniform Commission Examination process. The study is underway and the consultant will provide recommendations for coordinating the two processes. New examiners hired by the OTS in 2010 have accepted positions with the OCC beginning in January 2011, and the agencies plan to enroll additional OTS employees in OCC national bank examiner training courses prior to the transfer date. Ultimately, the OCC's National Bank Examiner commission will expand to ensure that each commissioned examiner has the skill set and credentials to lead examinations of both national banks and federal savings associations.

3.1.3. Review of OTS Regulations (OCC)

The OCC has begun a comprehensive review of all of the OTS's regulations regarding savings associations. Working together with OTS staff, the OCC is in the process of considering how to integrate the OTS's regulations with the OCC's regulations. This process is expected to include certain changes that would be effective as of the July 21, 2011, transfer date and to continue in phases after the transfer date. Any substantive changes proposed to be made to either the OCC's or the OTS's regulations affecting savings associations will be published in the Federal Register.

3.2. Transfer of Authority and Responsibilities Regarding Oversight of State Savings Associations (FDIC)

Section 312(b)(2)(C) of Dodd-Frank transfers the supervisory responsibility for state-chartered savings associations to the FDIC. As of the date of enactment, there were 61 state-chartered savings associations. The FDIC is working closely with the OTS to execute an orderly transfer of authority and responsibility to ensure that effective supervision continues for these institutions both during and after the transition period. FDIC and OTS supervisory personnel have reviewed

2011 examination schedules and have agreed on an appropriate division of responsibility for the timely and effective completion of all scheduled examinations.

The OTS will have responsibility, along with the appropriate state, for scheduled 2011 examinations of state-chartered savings associations that can be completed prior to the transfer date. For the remaining examinations, the OTS and the FDIC will develop plans for a coordinated transfer of responsibility to the FDIC. Officials of both agencies are confident that there will be no gaps in the supervision of these institutions and that the supervisory approach for these institutions will continue to be rigorous, consistent, and balanced both during and after the transition.

After the transfer date, the FDIC will fully incorporate supervision of state-chartered savings associations into its supervisory program. Given their current size and condition, the FDIC expects to absorb all state-chartered savings associations into the appropriate FDIC Regional Office supervisory program. The following procedures will ensure an orderly transition of supervisory responsibilities from the OTS to the FDIC:

- At least monthly prior to the transfer date, the FDIC Regional Offices will coordinate with their OTS Regional Office counterparts regarding examination plans and scheduling for state-chartered savings associations.
- To the extent that state-chartered savings associations are currently under formal or informal enforcement action, or are expected to be placed under such action, the OTS will coordinate with the appropriate FDIC Regional Office to facilitate the effective transfer of oversight and monitoring of enforcement programs. Beginning in January 2011, the OTS will advise the FDIC of the development of any new formal or informal enforcement actions for state-chartered savings associations.
- Prior to the transfer date, the FDIC will participate in the examination of all state-chartered savings associations with total assets over \$1 billion or with a composite CAMELS rating of "3" or lower. If an institution is expected to be downgraded to "3" or lower, the OTS will inform the appropriate FDIC office of the examination plan, the assignment of ratings, and any follow-up supervisory program.

The FDIC and the OTS are both committed to the orderly transfer of caseload knowledge and responsibility. The FDIC will have new portfolio assignments in place on the transfer date. To that end, both agencies will ensure that the transfer of institutional knowledge and supervisory strategies for each transferred institution occurs within the six-month period prior to the transfer date. The FDIC will be responsible for maintaining OTS historical records for these institutions and, where necessary, will implement strategies to add required information on state-chartered thrifts into FDIC supervisory systems as quickly as possible. The FDIC does not anticipate transferring any of OTS's supervisory systems, although it may rely upon the OCC to maintain such systems and make the data on state-chartered thrifts available to the FDIC for a short period of time after the transfer date.

3.2.1. Transfer of OTS Examination Staff (FDIC)

The FDIC is working closely with the OTS and the OCC to identify the number of new examiner positions that will be required to perform the supervisory functions being transferred from the OTS to the FDIC as well as other FDIC examiner vacancies in locations where OTS examination staff are currently assigned. OTS employees will be given the opportunity to express interest in these positions, and if selected, will transfer to the FDIC not later than 90 days after July 21, 2011, as part of the transfer of function. The FDIC will fully integrate these employees into the

FDIC's existing organizational structure, and will assign responsibility for examinations and other supervisory activities for each state-chartered savings association to the appropriate FDIC field office on the transfer date.

3.2.2. Training and Certification of Employees (FDIC)

The FDIC has historically recognized and accepted professional examination credentials from other federal banking agencies, including the OTS. Accordingly, the FDIC will treat as commissioned FDIC examiners all OTS examiners who transfer to the FDIC with OTS accreditation. The FDIC will address any individual training gaps that emerge after the transfer date through individual training and development plans.

3.3. Transfer of Authority and Responsibilities Regarding Oversight of Savings and Loan Holding Companies (FRB)

Dodd-Frank transfers authority for consolidated supervision of Savings and Loan Holding Companies (SLHCs) and their non-depository subsidiaries from the OTS to the FRB effective July 21, 2011.

The FRB is engaged in a range of activities to implement this transfer. The FRB staff is working closely with the OTS, whose staff is providing valuable information, expertise, and consultation during this transition period. Additionally, the FRB is working with staff at the OCC and FDIC in light of the critical role that the primary federal regulator plays in contributing to the agency's knowledge of consolidated holding companies. The overriding principles guiding this work include securing an orderly transfer of information and knowledge, ensuring that there are no gaps in holding company supervision, and providing the thrift industry with information on a flow basis so as to increase certainty and minimize unnecessary disruption during the transition period. The FRB has a well developed supervisory program for the comprehensive consolidated supervision of U.S. bank holding companies (BHCs). The FRB's supervisory authorities in this regard are based in the Bank Holding Company Act (BHC Act) as enhanced by Dodd-Frank. The FRB has adopted supervisory guidance entitled, "Consolidated Supervision of Bank Holding Companies and the Combined U.S. Operations of Foreign Banking Organizations" (per SR letter 09-9/CA 08-12, www.federalreserve.gov/boarddocs/srletters/2008/SR0809.htm) that sets forth the supervisory approach and the corresponding program for holding company supervision.

The FRB believes that it is important that any company that controls a depository institution be held to appropriate standards of capitalization, liquidity, and risk management. Consequently, the FRB intends to the greatest extent possible, taking into account any unique characteristics of SLHCs and the requirements of HOLA, to carry out supervisory oversight of SLHCs on a comprehensive consolidated basis, consistent with the FRB's established approach regarding BHC supervision. To this end, FRB staff is reviewing all elements of its BHC supervision program to determine whether and how to incorporate SLHCs into the program, consistent with HOLA. The program includes understanding the structure of holding companies and activities of material parts of these companies; evaluating risks posed by non-banking activities in a holding company structure; imposing prudential standards on a consolidated basis; and assessing the consumer compliance risk profile for holding companies. As the FRB develops plans for other aspects of Dodd-Frank, it will extend these existing approaches to the supervisory programs for SLHCs as appropriate.

Dodd-Frank gives the FRB the authority to require grandfathered unitary SLHCs conducting activities other than financial activities to establish an intermediate holding company over all or a portion of the financial activities. The FRB has established a working group to consider the issues associated with this authority and its potential advantages to effective supervision of such grandfathered companies. The FRB will carry out any implementation of this authority only after a proposed rule has been published for notice and public comment.

The FRB anticipates that all regulations as appropriate, relating to supervision of SLHCs and non-depository institution subsidiaries of SLHCs and to transactions with affiliates; extensions of credit to executive officers, directors, and principal shareholders; and tying arrangements will continue and will be enforceable by the appropriate agency. A working group is conducting an analysis of OTS and FRB regulations and guidance documents to determine policy or technical differences, and to assess whether there are any gaps. The FRB will make the decision about which OTS regulations should be amended after the transfer date in conjunction with a broad assessment of the holding company standards to be applied to SLHCs and other policy considerations. The FRB will make changes to any transferred OTS regulations after public notice and opportunity for comment when necessary and appropriate.

The FRB and the OTS are engaged in detailed discussions on the range of operational issues that they need to address during the transition period. The OTS staff has provided information on its holding company program, and on current supervisory issues, in addition to detailed briefings on legal and regulatory issues. The agencies signed a memorandum of understanding (MOU) to facilitate the sharing of confidential supervisory information during the transition so that FRB staff can become familiar with the condition of each SLHC coming under its jurisdiction and to identify resource requirements needed on the transfer date. The FRB will integrate SLHCs into its existing programs that align institutions with institutional portfolios based on their size and complexity. For instance, smaller, noncomplex SLHCs will be supervised in the Community Banking Organization portfolio while larger, more complex SLHCs will be supervised in the Regional or Large Banking Organization portfolios. The FRB has assigned each SLHC to a responsible Reserve Bank (per SR letter 05-27 / CA letter 05-11, "Responsible Reserve Bank and Inter-District Coordination"). To facilitate the transition process, and pursuant to the MOU, examiners from the FRB are joining certain OTS examinations prior to the transfer date to gather information and learn about the OTS supervisory process. Discussions are well underway about the orderly transition of the caseload from the OTS to the Reserve Banks.

3.4. Continuation of Thrift Industry Reporting Requirements

The agencies have reviewed whether savings associations should continue filing the Thrift Financial Report (TFR) and have determined, subject to public notice and comment and OMB approval, that it would be best to phase out the separate collection of TFR data and to merge that data collection process into the Call Report process used by other FDIC-insured depository institutions beginning with the March 2012 reporting period. The OTS, the OCC, the FRB, and the FDIC, under the auspices of the Federal Financial Institutions Examination Council (FFIEC), have worked together closely and plan to publish a joint notice in the Federal Register in the near future, with a request for comments regarding burden estimates and how best to accomplish this change. Non-OTS regulated financial institutions (including all national banks) currently submit the Call Report using the FFIEC's Central Data Repository (CDR), which is published using the CDR's Public Data Distribution Web site.

The agencies have further agreed that the FDIC will assume responsibility for TFR reporting on an interim basis beginning with the second quarter 2011 TFR. To ensure a smooth transition, OTS personnel who are assigned to the TFR reporting and data analysis functions will begin working with the FDIC during the second quarter 2011 TFR data collection process as soon as the first quarter 2011 TFR reporting process has been completed. These staff will transfer to the FDIC no later than 90 days after the transfer date to support the transition of thrifts to the Call Report and the ongoing reporting process for these institutions. In addition, OTS personnel who are assigned to the FDIC will continue to process all of the existing SLHC reports that are currently required to be filed by the OTS through December 31, 2011.

To ensure that the FDIC has adequate staff to analyze conditions in the banking industry after the thrifts begin to report data through the Call Report process, a portion of the OTS staff in Washington, D.C., who currently use the TFR data to analyze conditions in the economy and the thrift industry will transfer to the FDIC no later than 90 days after the transfer date to perform similar functions for the FDIC. The OTS personnel who currently operate and maintain the systems that support the TFR process will transfer to the OCC on the transfer date, but will be responsible for temporarily maintaining the infrastructure to support ongoing data collection activities for the TFR. If there is a transition of thrift reporting to the Call Report process in 2012, this infrastructure will no longer be used to collect TFR data.

In conjunction with the transition of the TFR to the Call Report process, the agencies have also agreed that it would be best to phase out production of the separate Uniform Thrift Performance Report (UTPR). Once thrifts transition to submitting Call Report data, a Uniform Bank Performance Report (UBPR) will automatically be produced for them.

The OTS and the FDIC have also agreed that it would be best to cease OTS collection of the Branch Office Survey (BOS) after 2010. Beginning with the 2011 data collection, thrifts would submit branch office data using the FDIC's Summary of Deposits (SOD) system. The agencies will need to do minimal work on the SOD system to ensure that it can collect the data beginning in July 2011. The OTS and the FDIC plan to publish a notice in the Federal Register in the near future, with a request for comments on how best to accomplish this change.

The agencies recognize that TFR, UTPR, and BOS historical data needs to be maintained for an indeterminate period to ensure continued accessibility for the public and the agencies. To the extent that this information is stored in existing OTS systems, the OCC will have this responsibility after the transfer date.

Finally, the FRB evaluated the continued use of the consolidated thrift holding company information in the TFR, the continued use of other regulatory reports in the current SLHC reporting scheme, and whether SLHCs should submit more comprehensive consolidated reports as well as a comprehensive parent company only report in a manner consistent with those reports submitted by BHCs. The FRB is in the process of issuing a separate notice of its intentions to phase out the current SLHC reporting scheme and to require SLHCs to adopt reporting standards and processes required of all FRB-regulated BHCs. According to plans, the current SLHC reporting scheme would continue in place through 2011, and the new reporting requirements would take effect beginning with the March 2012 reporting period. The FRB plans to publish a notice in the Federal Register with request for comment regarding burden estimates later this year. In addition, the FRB worked closely with the other banking agencies as they deliberated on the appropriate reporting requirements of the subsidiary savings associations with the intention of providing as much consistency in reporting as appropriate between the reporting of the subsidiary savings associations and the SLHCs. The FRB is also evaluating the need for organizational structure data of SLHCs and the collection of this information into the FRB's structure database.

3.5. Continuation of Suits

All actions or proceedings commenced by or against the OTS or the Director of the OTS prior to the transfer date are continued by Dodd-Frank. The OCC, the FDIC, and the FRB will be substituted as parties for such actions, consistent with the transfer of functions, on or after the transfer date.

The agencies will review and inventory all litigation files of the OTS and determine which agency under Dodd-Frank has the supervisory jurisdiction over a specific case based on the regulatory plaintiff or defendant named in the action or would have responsibility for the subject matter of the suit if it were brought after the effective transfer date. Staff from each agency will inventory existing suits and create a master list of cases that includes reference to the receiving supervisory agency. The OTS will furnish the case file and associated documents to the receiving agency on or before the transfer date. Cases with co-parties that may involve dual regulatory oversight under Dodd-Frank shall be assigned to the appropriate supervisory agencies. "Suits" include administrative or court actions such as civil money penalties against companies, associations, or individuals; supervisory agreements; orders enforcing safety and soundness standards; prompt corrective action directives; cease and desist orders; temporary cease and desist orders; removal and prohibition orders; injunctive actions; temporary suspensions; as well as cases against the OTS involving all pending court reviews of agency action, including challenges to rules or orders, and Freedom of Information Act actions.

The OCC or the FDIC will handle employment actions that involve OTS employees who are transferred to the OCC or the FDIC, respectively. The OCC will handle employment actions that involve former OTS employees who have not transferred to the OCC or the FDIC.

3.6. Continuation of Existing Orders, Resolutions, Determinations, Agreements, Regulations, etc.

All orders, resolutions, determinations, agreements, regulations, interpretive rules, other interpretations, guidelines, procedures, and other advisory materials that have been issued by the OTS, or a court of competent jurisdiction, in the performance of functions transferred by Dodd-Frank that are in effect on the day before the transfer date will continue to remain in effect according to their terms. These materials will be enforceable by or against the OCC, the FDIC, and the FRB, as appropriate, consistent with the transfer of functions until modified, terminated, set aside, or superseded by an appropriate agency, court of competent jurisdiction, or operation of law.

3.6.1. Identification of Regulations Continued

Dodd-Frank requires the OCC, the FDIC, and the FRB to identify those continued OTS regulations that each agency will enforce. The OCC and the FDIC must consult with each other in identifying these regulations, and the OCC, the FRB, and the FDIC must publish a list of these identified regulations in the Federal Register not later than the transfer date. The agencies have begun the task of identifying these OTS regulations and will publish the lists required by the legislation on or before the transfer date.

3.6.2. Status of Regulations Proposed or Not Yet Effective

Any regulation proposed by the OTS in performing functions transferred by Dodd-Frank that has not been published as a final regulation before the transfer date will be considered to be a proposed regulation of the OCC or the FRB, as appropriate, according to the terms of the proposed regulation. Any interim or final regulation that the OTS published prior to the transfer date in performing functions transferred by Dodd-Frank but which has not become effective before the transfer date will become effective as a regulation of the OCC or the FRB, as appropriate, according to the terms of such regulation, unless modified, terminated or set aside, or superseded by the OCC or the FRB, as appropriate, or by a court of competent jurisdiction or operation of law.

4. Transfer of Funds

Section 4 of this plan describes the effective transfer of funds from the OTS to the OCC. The FDIC and the FRB have determined that no funds will be transferred from the OTS to their respective agencies.

4.1. Transfer of Funds

The OCC, the FDIC, the FRB, and the OTS have established a workgroup to address the transfer of funds that, on the day before the transfer date, the Director of the OTS determines are not necessary to dispose of the OTS's affairs, under section 325 of Dodd-Frank, and are available to the OTS to pay its expenses relating to the agency's functions that are transferred under section 312(b). Some of the more significant concerns that the workgroup will address include the appropriate distribution of the OTS investment portfolio holdings, its reserves, and any real property (see separate discussion in Section 5.1). The workgroup will also establish a framework for the distribution of OTS funds.

The OCC will incorporate the OTS account balances transferred to the OCC into the OCC's trial balance operating accounts on the transfer date. The OTS agency location code and associated fund symbols will remain open at the Department of the Treasury (Treasury) pending clearance of all outstanding transactions. When all known outstanding transactions have cleared through Treasury, the OCC will initiate procedures to close the OTS Treasury accounts.

4.2. Funding: Establishing an Assessment Process

4.2.1. OCC

The OCC and the OTS receive their primary source of funding through fees, also known as assessments, received from the institutions under their supervision. Both agencies collect these assessments twice a year to fund their operations. The assessment each financial institution pays generally relates to the total dollar amount of assets under supervision and reflects the cost to supervise the industry as a whole, as opposed to the cost of supervising any one particular bank or thrift.

Since the assessment process is the primary means of funding for the OCC and the OTS, the OCC and the OTS established a joint Bank Assessment Workgroup (BAW) on July 26, 2010. The membership of the workgroup includes experienced economics, legal, and financial management staff. The members meet at least monthly and have developed a project plan to guide the work of the BAW and to develop recommendations for the Comptroller of the Currency's consideration. The OCC will continue to monitor the OCC's short- and long-term funding needs and make decisions concerning assessments as required. Currently, the financial condition of the OCC is not expected to significantly change as a result of integrating the resources needed to perform OTS functions.

4.2.2. FDIC

Consistent with its current practice for the state non-member insured depository institutions for which it is the primary federal supervisor, the FDIC does not intend to charge assessments for its supervision of state-chartered savings associations.

4.2.3. FRB

Section 318(c) of Dodd-Frank directs the FRB to collect a total amount of assessments, fees, or other charges from (1) all BHCs with total consolidated assets of $50 billion or more, (2) all SLHCs with total consolidated assets of $50 billion or more, and (3) all nonbank financial companies supervised by the FRB under section 113 of Dodd-Frank that is equal to the total expenses the FRB estimates are necessary or appropriate to carry out the supervisory and regulatory responsibilities of the FRB with respect to such companies.

The FRB is directed to offset only a portion of its total supervision and regulation costs—that is, only the portion attributed to those institutions that meet the criteria described above. This portion of the FRB's total supervision and regulation costs will be offset through assessment fees charged to these institutions. With respect to SLHCs, only those with assets equal to or above $50 billion will be subject to assessment. Those SLHCs with assets less than $50 billion will not be subject to a supervision assessment of the holding company.

To implement this section of Dodd-Frank, the FRB will (1) identify and quantify the total respective costs necessary or appropriate to carry out the supervisory or regulatory responsibilities with respect to these companies (2) formulate a framework to apportion these costs to these companies through periodic assessment fees, and (3) implement a process to collect the assessments. A team comprised of staff from the FRB's divisions of Banking Supervision and Regulation, Management, Legal, and Reserve Bank Operations Efforts are responsible for implementing these supervision assessment fees.

Initial efforts to identify the applicable supervision and regulation costs associated with these companies are underway. The FRB is considering a variety of approaches to differentiate these costs from total supervision. The FRB plans to provide notice for establishing the framework for the assessments before the collection of assessments in 2012.

5. Transfer of Property

Section 5 of this plan describes the process for transferring all owned and leased real property, personal property and all associated furniture, fixtures, equipment, reports of examination, work papers, files, papers, and any other information and materials from the OTS to the OCC, the FDIC, and the FRB pursuant to Section 323 of Dodd-Frank. The OTS is committed to making a thorough, complete, and transparent inventory and disposition of all OTS property to the appropriate receiving agencies.

The agencies will complete property transfer no later than 90 days after the transfer date.

5.1. Transfer of the OTS Building and Real Property

Section 323(b)(1) of Dodd-Frank provides that all real property, including the OTS headquarters building and associated real estate, will transfer to the OCC or the FDIC in a manner consistent with the transfer of OTS employees. The agencies have jointly determined that ownership of all buildings and real property will transfer to the OCC. The FDIC will house transferring OTS employees in current FDIC facilities. The OCC's legal staff are working to determine appropriate transfers of title and transfers of leases to the OCC effective July 21, 2011.

5.2. Transfer of Information Technology Assets, Systems, and Infrastructure

Dodd-Frank provides that OTS Information Technology (IT) assets, systems, and infrastructure will be transferred to the OCC, the FDIC, or the FRB consistent with Section 323.

The OCC, FDIC, and OTS Chief Information Officers are working closely together to develop a plan to integrate the agencies' assets and systems. The combined business needs drive the plan to meet short-term transition objectives and long-term integration goals. The agencies will follow applicable policies and procedures to ensure that all assets are transferred in a structured and secure manner to support transferred functions and personnel.

5.2.1. OCC

The OCC and the OTS have developed an analysis framework and completed a comprehensive inventory of IT assets and systems by business function. Using this framework as a guide, OCC staff is analyzing both agencies' systems, from the business and technical perspective, to recommend the best course of action for each system with the goals of integrating and aligning business and reducing duplication as much and as quickly as possible. To minimize the potential impact on personnel and regulated entities, the OCC anticipates that some information systems may need to run in parallel for an initial period to ensure continuity and availability.

The plan will also ensure that core OCC administrative systems and IT infrastructure services, such as time and attendance and e-mail, are available to all incoming OTS staff by the transfer date. For other OTS administrative systems and infrastructure services being retired, the end of the fiscal year or beyond may be a more appropriate timeframe for transition. The OCC will allot sufficient time for training OTS and OCC employees on any new systems as necessary.

5.2.2. FDIC

FDIC and OTS staff will work together to determine how best to integrate supervisory and administrative information from OTS systems into existing FDIC automated information systems, with a goal of accomplishing this transition as quickly as possible. The staff will also develop guidelines for the retention and archiving of relevant OTS data to ensure that it continues to be available, as needed, in the future.

The FDIC does not anticipate transferring from the OTS any IT systems, equipment, or other infrastructure. To ensure compatibility, the FDIC will issue standard FDIC IT equipment and software to all OTS employees transferring to the FDIC.

5.2.3. FRB

The FRB is working with the OTS on direct access to its systems and official records (including supervisory ratings, enforcement actions, other assessments, examination reports and related work papers, application filings, and all other communications with SLHCs), to the extent consistent with the Dodd-Frank, other applicable law, and other legal constraints. The FRB also has access to comprehensive OTS databases containing structure and financial data. The FRB is also working with the FDIC and the OCC to ensure comprehensive bilateral information sharing and coordination for thrift subsidiaries comparable to that in place for BHC bank subsidiaries.

Staff from the OTS and the FRB also are working toward automated information transfers of the key SLHC and subsidiary structure data to the FRB. In addition, the interagency team will handle the supervisory information requirements in a similar manner, preparing for automated transfers of OTS key supervisory information to the FRB to be incorporated in FRB automated systems. The banking agencies are working through the FFIEC Task Force for Information Sharing and its workgroups.

5.2.4. TFR Reporting Systems

The OCC, the OTS, and the FDIC are working together to determine disposition of the system supporting the TFR process, consistent with the joint proposal to phase out separate collection of the TFR in 2012 (see section 3.4).

5.3. Transfer of Records

By the transfer date, the OTS will update and verify inventories and locations of paper and electronic records for both current, active records as well as archived records. Consistent with Section 323 of Dodd-Frank, OTS records and information regarding OTS functions and activities will be transferred to the OCC, the FDIC, and the FRB.

The OTS, OCC, and FDIC records management staffs have established a joint team that is working to identify the types of records and the related comprehensive records schedules for both agencies, and to identify and catalogue the number and physical location of all records. The team is working directly with the National Archives and Records Administration (NARA) to determine how best to establish a new, joint comprehensive records schedule for the OCC and its expanded responsibilities. Team members are jointly preparing a plan for physically transferring OTS records, as appropriate, to OCC, FDIC, and FRB recordkeeping facilities, NARA facilities, and the Federal Records Centers.

Similarly, the FRB has established a team, which includes staff from across the Federal Reserve System, to coordinate the transfer of records with the OTS. The effort includes identifying records that the FRB will need to perform or support the supervisory authority being transferred to the FRB. The FRB is coordinating closely with the OTS to complete the transfer of records. The implementation plan for the official transfer will have a dependency based on the volume, format, and physical location of OTS records identified for the transfer. The FRB has notified

Reserve Bank Districts that the official transfer of records is being coordinated nationally by FRB staff.

5.4. Transferring Contracts

The OTS has recently updated and verified inventories of all open and active leases of real and personal property, purchase orders, and contracts. Consistent with Section 323, OTS leases, purchase orders, and contracts will transfer to the OCC. The FDIC does not anticipate assuming responsibility for any OTS leases, contracts, or purchase orders.

For contracts transferring to the OCC, the OCC's Acquisition Management staff (Acquisitions) will review all active actions to identify and address any redundancies. During the review, Acquisitions will work with the OTS to determine which contracts provide the OCC the best support and represent the best value. The OCC will consider the following factors during the review:

- Contract terms and conditions,
- Rights of the government pertaining to increased quantities or scope,
- Periods of performance and remaining option periods,
- Termination provisions,
- Performance issues,
- Cost and price, and
- Available funding.

Once a decision is made regarding which contracts best support the OCC after the transfer date, Acquisitions will take the necessary steps to execute appropriate modifications. The OCC's Administrative and Internal Law Department staff will review contract modification actions for legal sufficiency, as necessary.

5.5. Transfer of Other Assets

All other OTS assets not otherwise identified in this report that come to light during the wind down of the OTS will be inventoried, recorded, and transferred to the OCC, the FDIC, and the FRB in accordance with Section 323 of Dodd-Frank. The FDIC and the FRB have determined that they do not require any additional assets not described above from the OTS.

The OCC also recently completed an inventory of accountable property and has updated its Asset Management (AM) system to reflect the current status. The OTS plans to conduct a complete inventory in the April/May 2011 timeframe of all its accountable property. Once that effort is completed, the OCC will enter the appropriate assets into its AM system for continued accountability.

6. Other Recommendations and Actions

Section 6 describes other recommendations and actions to ensure an orderly and effective process.

6.1. Communication with the Industry

The agencies recognize the importance of communicating regularly with the industry throughout this process. Among other things, the agencies are developing an outreach program for thrift executives to provide information and perspective on their approach to supervision and regulation. The agencies will hold these programs at various locations throughout the country. An OCC District Deputy Comptroller and an OTS Regional Director will co-host events for federal savings associations. Participation will include FRB representatives. During these sessions, senior examiners will explain how the agencies examine banks and BHCs, including the development of individually tailored supervisory strategies based on the unique risks facing each institution. The program also will describe the functions of the OCC's district counsel and district licensing activities as well as the FRB's application process. The agencies expect these events to take place in the first and second quarters of 2011. The acting Comptroller of the Currency also sent a personal letter to the chief executive officers of each federal savings association to begin the process of communication that will be important throughout the transition.

The FDIC, the OTS, and relevant state authorities will host similar events in areas where state-chartered savings associations have a significant presence.

In addition to the thrift-focused programs, OCC, FRB, FDIC, and OTS supervision managers will continue to participate in industry events that provide interaction with thrift executives in group settings as well as individual conversations to expand the industry's awareness of the agencies' policies, procedures, and supervision philosophy.

6.2. Labor Relations

The OCC and the OTS have invited union representatives to participate in agency planning team meetings. A union representative attends meetings, reviews correspondence, and interacts with management on a pre-decisional basis on an array of activities in support of implementation of sections 301-326 of Dodd-Frank.

The FDIC is providing periodic updates to its employee union on the status of the transition.

6.3 Disposition of OTS Affairs

The OTS Acting Director and a small cadre of staff will make a final disposition of the affairs of the OTS during the 90-day period after the transfer date. The OTS will use this period to ensure a full and accurate accounting and transfer of all OTS human resources, assets, and property of all kinds. The OTS will ensure that compensation and benefits owed to OTS employees will be provided and will prudently manage remaining property and assets until transfer. The OTS intends to take actions to make an appropriate disposition of its affairs and document the measures taken to wind down the agency.